the *sego*

the segovia technique

by vladimir bobri

THE BOLD STRUMMER. LTD.

20 TURKEY HILL CIRCLE / BOX 2037
WESTPORT CONNECTICUT 06880

acknowledgments

My deepest gratitude to the following members of the editorial board of
the *Guitar Review*, without whose help this book could never have been completed:

SAUL MARANTZ
who took most of the photographs and spent hours in the darkroom experimenting
with prints to achieve a maximum of brilliance and clarity

GEORGE GIUSTI
for the delightful line drawings on pages 15, 34, and 81, and an important photograph on page 47

MICHAEL KASHA
who provided material on the Hittite and Athenian guitars

MARTHA NELSON
for general research work and invaluable help in editing and preparing the text
to conform visually to the original design of the book

ANTONIO PETRUCCELLI
for his help in preparation of layouts and for expert retouching of photographs

FRANZ C. HESS
who made the typographical realization of the original layout

GREGORY D'ALESSIO
for a critical reading of the text

and most of all

ANDRES SEGOVIA
who, after infecting me some forty years ago with *virus guitaristicus*,
became my friend and mentor. To him I give thanks for his continuing encouragement
of the entire project, careful correction of the text, especially
the technical parts, and his patient suffering for hours in the heat of
summer under the photographer's hot lights.

ISBN 0-933224-49-4

contents

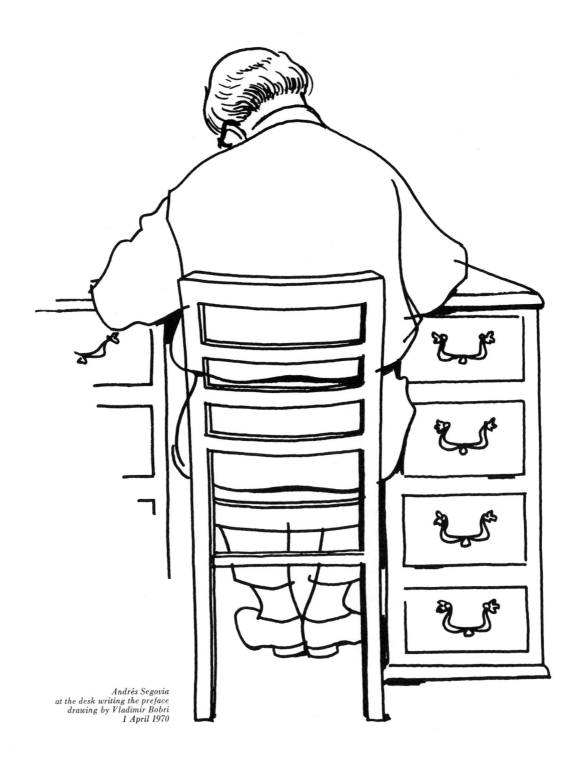

Andrés Segovia
at the desk writing the preface
drawing by Vladimir Bobri
1 April 1970

In designing a building, the architect makes sure that its foundation is sufficiently solid to support the weight of the entire structure. Similarly, in learning to play the guitar, the student must first establish the foundation of his technique. Only when his posture, his way of holding the instrument, position and action of both hands are correct will he find himself able to solve the progressive difficulties of his studies in a musically acceptable way. This book, written and illustrated by one of my best friends in the United States, who also possesses a thorough knowledge of the guitar, deals exclusively with the problem of establishing the preliminary foundation of proper guitar technique. Teachers and students will find in this book a comprehensive collection of photographs and drawings illustrating efficient advice as to how to hold the instrument, how to put the right hand in the right position, and also how to achieve the correct action of the left so that the right may produce beautiful tones and achieve a fluent technique. The study of works of Aguado, Sor, Giuliani, Carulli, Tárrega, and later on Villa-Lobos can be undertaken more successfully with this preliminary study.

The author showing Segovia an enlarged diagrammatic representation of the maestro's right hand playing position

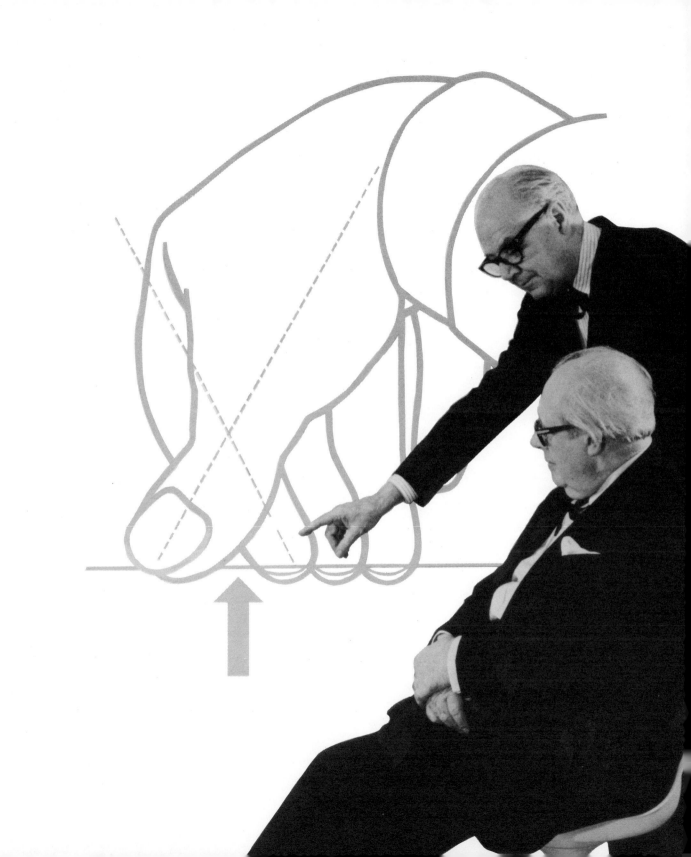

classic guitar
historical outline

The following pages show
a few high points in the slow but inexorable development
of the instrument from its primitive antecedents to today's concert guitar.

hittite guitar

*The guitar 3300 years ago,
on a Hittite stone carving from
Alaja Huyuk, now in Ankara Arkeoloji Muzesi
Photograph courtesy Michael Kasha,
Florida State University*

2

hittite guitar

This remarkable stone carving is among the earliest known representations of a plucked string instrument that has all of the essential elements of a guitar. This stone relief is from the Sphinx gate and city walls of the New Hittite Empire settlement at Alaja Huyuk, dating from about 1400-1350 B.C. (The Hittites were early Indo-European language-group settlers and conquerors of the Anatolian Peninsula, and are thought to have migrated from the Caucasus.) The long neck with frets, the incurved sides or ribs on a flat body, the array of soundholes on each side of the neck, all serve to classify the instrument as an ancient ancestor of the classic guitar. The presence of the long neck continuing through the length of the body is typical of plucked instruments of that era, as also seen on Egyptian "long lutes" of that period; similarly the array of soundholes resembles that on some Egyptian instruments. The Hittites were in contact with the Egyptians, and these common elements are not surprising. Another interesting comparison can be made with the "Guitarra Latina" illustrated in the c. A.D. 1270 Spanish manuscript, *Cantigas de Santa María de Alfonso el Sabio* (*Guitar Review* 29, 1966, p. 6, left), which has some features remarkably similar to this Hittite guitar of some 2700 years earlier, especially the arrangement of soundholes.

The Hittite guitarist is apparently using a plectrum hung from a ribbon attached to his belt buckle and has decorated his guitar with ribbons flowing from the head of the instrument. It seems that even in those days a warped guitar neck was sometimes observed.

Athenian guitarist, 400 B.C.,

Athens National Museum

Photograph courtesy

Michael Kasha

4

athenian guitar

Archeological evidence shows that guitar-like instruments were known to the northern Mediterranean peoples, including the Greeks and Romans. It is thus possible to trace a slow migration and development of the guitar to the Iberian Peninsula along the northern Mediterranean, until the "Guitarra Latina" of the thirteenth-century Cantigas.

This Athenian plays with a hand technique remarkably similar to that now used by the classic guitarist. When Segovia saw this picture, he remarked: "I might well have derived my technique from her!"

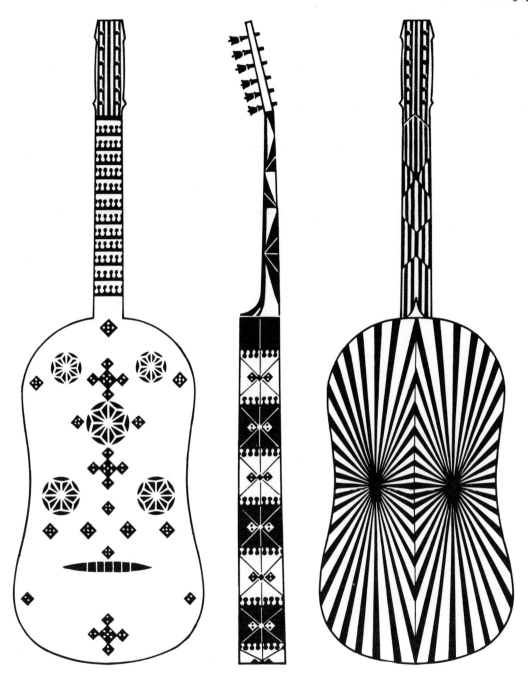

vihuela, c. 1500, Spain

Orpheus plays a six-course vihuela in the frontispiece of Luys Milán's El Maestro, *published in Valencia, 1535. This first great collection of works for vihuela gives us a rich heritage of exquisite music often included today in the concert repertoire of the guitar. Photograph courtesy of the Biblioteca Nacional, Madrid*

vihuela

The vihuela was a direct predecessor of the guitar. The drawing shows an instrument in the Musée Jacquemart-André, Paris, which was made around 1500. On the side of the tuning head appears the word *Guadalupe,* the burned-in imprint of the Monastery of Guadalupe in Estremadura, Spain. The vihuela had six courses of strings, each course consisting of two strings tuned in unison or octaves. It flourished during an age of great polyphonic music and of superb virtuosos who could improvise the most elaborate counterpoint.

italian guitar

This Italian guitar, from the collection of W. E. Hill and Son, London luthiers, displays another step in guitar evolution. The soundboard extends a distance of three frets onto the fingerboard, set flush with it. The last frets are set directly into the soundboard. The soundhole is open, and the instrument still has five double courses, but its silhouette begins to approach that of the contemporary classic guitar. A considerable body of music for this type of guitar survives. Robert de Visée, guitarist to the court of Louis XIV, left numerous original compositions, much admired in guitar concerts today.

9 *Dame de qualité jouant de la Guitarre. French engraving, c. 1694, collection V. Bobri*

Carulli guitar

In 1810 Ferdinando Carulli, famed for his guitar compositions and his virtuosity, presented this beautiful Italian instrument to his thirteen-year-old son Gustave, who later bequeathed it to the Musée du Conservatoire National de Musique, Paris, while he was a professor there. Whereas various types of stringing had been used on the classic guitar (four double courses; five double courses; six courses consisting of five double and one single, etc.), the Carulli guitar has the same *accordatura* used today: six single strings, tuned E-A-d-g-b-e[1].

Antonio Torres

This guitar was made in 1863 by one of the great modern luthiers, Antonio Torres Jurado. Torres, as he is more commonly known to the guitar world, was born in San Sebastian de Almería, Spain, on 13 June 1817 and died there on 19 November 1892. His work marks a major step in the development of the classic guitar.

Perhaps the most important contribution of Torres was establishing the string length of 650 mm., which subsequently became the standard of all modern guitars. This naturally set the size and proportions of the body of the guitar as well as the length of the fingerboard. The guitars of Torres have an elegance of outline rarely equaled even by his closest emulators and they all have one trait in common: extreme softness of touch and ease of action. More important, a definite tone quality is common to all Torres guitars—mellow, yet robust, and once heard, never forgotten.

Collection Rose L. Augustine

today's concert guitar

The classic guitar of today as played by Andrés Segovia preserves the characteristic figure-eight shape of its predecessors, but is somewhat larger and wider. Its wider fingerboard (a minimum of two inches at the nut) accommodates the strings without crowding or hampering the fingers in any way; there are twelve frets (or one octave) between the body of the instrument and its head, and six (sometimes seven) over the soundboard. The strings are attached to a flat bridge glued to the soundboard. The interior construction is characterized by a fan-shaped system of bracing under the soundboard, to give it maximum strength and vibrational elasticity. The entire instrument is made of the choicest seasoned woods, selected for resonance and strength; it is usually decorated with marquetry around the circular soundhole, and occasionally on other parts of the instrument.

The classic guitar, unlike most instruments, produces its sound through direct contact of the fingertips and nails, whence the suavity of sound and diversity of tone color. Its range is from E, two octaves below middle C, to B, an octave and a seventh above middle C. It is capable of realizing contrapuntal passages, full harmonies, and chords of up to six notes.

In *Guitar Review* 16 (1954), Segovia states, "Few realize the influence of the luthier on the life and career of the artist. Without the existence of an adequate instrument, the fantasy, the emotional richness, the technical precision and the essence of musical interpretation—all these would remain latent. They

Guitar by Hermann Hauser, 1940.
Collection Rose L. Augustine, New York

might never be revealed, or at best, be imperfectly revealed." Among the many excellent artisans of the past seventy years two luthiers are outstanding for having provided Segovia with instruments that he would cherish as perfect tools for his artistic career. The first was Manuel Ramirez (1869–1920), the Madrid maker whose instrument—Segovia's first really fine guitar—served him for many years. The second was the German craftsman, Hermann Hauser (1882–1952), who in 1936 created what Segovia in *Guitar Review* 16 called "THE GREATEST GUITAR OF OUR EPOCH." This instrument, now also at rest after more than fifteen years of travel with Segovia to all parts of the globe, can be heard in his recordings made for Decca Records during the 1940s and 1950s.

As a very young man, during the period 1910–1912, Segovia played an instrument made by Benito Ferrer. Then, in 1912, he acquired the Manuel Ramirez guitar already referred to, which was his constant companion until 1933. Beginning in 1933 and until 1956 he played instruments constructed especially for him by Hermann Hauser, and from 1956 to 1960 by Hermann Hauser, Jr. During the decade 1960–1970 he has added to his collection of principal instruments guitars by Ignacio Fleta, which he used between 1960 and 1963, and later by José Ramirez, Jr. Most of these makers have supplied Segovia with a number of instruments over a period of time, and dates given can be only approximate, since there has been much overlapping.

It is evident from this list that Segovia has no personal preference for individual luthiers. His choice is governed entirely by the quality of the instrument.

Guitar by José Ramirez, Jr., 1960.

Collection Andrés Segovia

strings

Albert Augustine (1900–1967)

When Segovia was a young boy the classic guitar was strung with three fine-quality gut strings and three silk-cored strings wound with fine silvered wire. These strings, though sweet in tone, cause the guitarist to endure great tribulations because of their unpredictability, their fragility, and their quick loss of resonance. The first strings Segovia used were made in Granada and bore the brand name *La Viuda.* Later he preferred strings made by Pirastro. Then, after suffering much anxiety because of a scarcity of strings during World War II, in 1947 he began a life-long friendship with one who was to put an end to Segovia's constant searching for a satisfactory guitar string. This was Albert Augustine, who, at Segovia's urging, was to develop, from plastic material obtained from the Du Pont company, nylon strings which were to replace the gut strings with incalculable advantage in durability, exact calibration, sound, and ease of action. Since 1947 Segovia has used the nylon mono-filament treble strings and the fine-wire wound nylon-cored bass strings manufactured by Albert Augustine Ltd. of New York.

virtuosi

The nineteenth century is often referred to as the Golden Age of the Guitar. Spaniards Dionisio Aguado (1784–1849) and Fernando Sor (1778–1839), together with Italians Matteo Carcassi (1792–1853), Mauro Giuliani (1781–1829), and Ferdinando Carulli (1770–1841), to name only the most outstanding, contributed greatly to the evolution of guitar technique. Virtuoso performers, they brought the guitar for the first time to concert performance level. Methods of study still in use today were published and much beautiful music was composed, some of it to become part of the standard guitar repertoire.

16

Dionisio Aguado (1784–1849). Portrait from his Nuevo Método para Guitarra, *published in Paris and Madrid 1843*

Fernando Sor (1778–1839)

Portrait by J. Goubaud, engraved by M. N. Bate

Photograph by Roger Viollet, Paris

17

Ferdinando Carulli (1770–1841)

Lithograph by G. Engelmann

Matteo Carcassi (1702 1853)
Portrait by Jules David
Photograph from the
Bibliothèque Nationale, Paris,
courtesy The Art
and Times of the Guitar,
by Frederic V. Grunfeld

Mauro Giuliani (1781–1829)

Portrait by Stubenrauch, engraved by Jugel

The popularity of the guitar was tremendous,

as this lively altercation between the followers of Ferdinando Carulli and Francisco Molino shows.

Lithograph from La Guitaromanie *by Charles de Marescot. Photograph courtesy la Bibliothèque Nationale, Paris*

FRANCISCO TARREGA
1852-1909

22

In the second half of the nineteenth century the extraordinary popularity of the guitar rapidly declined. Unskilled amateurs and salon singers had taken over. The guitar hung on the wall of the barber shop. The pianoforte began to dominate the concert stage.

Then, at the end of the nineteenth century, a small but devoted group of guitarists in many lands worked valiantly to preserve and improve on the achievements of the Golden Age. The great Spanish master Francisco Tárrega (1852–1909) continued the work of Aguado and Sor. He made an important contribution to the technique of the right hand, emphasizing the supported stroke (*apoyando*) and stressing the importance of the third finger of the right hand, until then somewhat neglected. Tárrega developed and rationalized the Spanish technique of tone production. He also wrote a series of highly important studies, laying the foundation for modern technique. The art of transcription for the guitar was brought by Tárrega to a new level of perfection, demonstrating the formidable resources of the instrument. Miguel Llobet (1878–1937) extended the work of Tárrega, leaving us a series of superb transcriptions fully utilizing the expressive delicacy of the guitar.

◀ *drawing by Grisha Dotzenko*
copyright 1953 by the Society of the Classic Guitar
used by permission

Andrés Segovia
27 February 1969
Photograph by Ken Richards

Andrés Segovia

Although both Tárrega and Llobet were accomplished performers and sensitive musicians, neither one possessed the temperament and brilliance of technique necessary to project the classic guitar successfully before the general public. This task was predestined for Andrés Segovia, in whose hands the guitar has been brought to a new position of musical prominence. Andrés Segovia has elevated the instrument to undreamed heights of technical mastery. His impeccable musical taste and musicianship have enabled him to produce a formidable array of transcriptions, creating a new guitar repertoire of classic and modern music. His genius has inspired composers of note, such as Manuel Ponce, Heitor Villa-Lobos, Alexandre Tansman, Mario Castelnuovo-Tedesco, Joaquín Rodrigo, Federico Moreno-Torroba, and Joaquín Turina, to name only a few, to write new and exciting works for his instrument. In addition, Segovia has explored successfully the possibilities of a guitarist as soloist with chamber and symphony orchestras, performing new and especially written works.

The impact of Segovia's innumerable concerts in virtually every country of the globe and countless recordings displaying his matchless musicianship has resulted in a veritable renaissance of the instrument. A new generation of young guitarists, inspired or directly taught by the master, are making their debuts on the concert stage; musical academies are establishing chairs of the guitar; societies of the classic guitar have been formed in all parts of the world. Magazines of high musical and artistic standards like *Guitar Review* have been published successfully since 1946. A veritable deluge of guitars, as well as music, methods, and instruction books for the classic guitar, is sold to millions of people.

It is inevitable that with such an abundance we are confronted with a great deal of conflicting and even worthless, if not harmful, advice and instructions for the beginners. The situation is further aggravated by a dearth of competent teachers. This situation is slowly improving, as students of Segovia mature and form a nucleus of competent teachers. But we deem it timely and necessary to have a clear and lucid explanation of Andrés Segovia's technique in a permanent and indisputable form.

With the help of the maestro himself, this picture book of the Segovia technique has been made possible. The author hopes that it will be not only an authoritative source of information and instruction, but also a pictorial record of the technique of the master who reestablished the dignity of the guitar in our century, elevating it to its proper role among the serious instruments of music.

at an early age in Granada

27

Portrait of Andrés Segovia—published by the Society of the Classic Guitar in 1959 to commemorate his fifty years on the concert stage

Designed by V. Bobri

Andrés Segovia was born on 21 February 1893 in Linares, a small mining town in the Andalusian province of Jaén. Shortly after his birth the family moved to Granada, which had been until 1492 the stronghold of the Moors on Spanish soil. There he was to spend his impressionable years. One of the young boy's favorite retreats was the Alhambra. The arabesqued walls of its palaces are still reflected in courtyard pools, amidst enchanting gardens, murmuring fountains and *miradores,* all guarded by massive saffron-colored towers that inspired Albéniz to write his famous *Torre Bermeja.* The tranquil beauty of the Alhambra perhaps played a part in awakening in Segovia an early appreciation of the arts.

To encourage the musically inclined Andresito, his family offered him piano, violin, or cello lessons from the available local "professors." However, neither these instruments nor the performers could capture his imagination. Already he was drawn to the guitar, which sounded so sweet to him even in the untrained hands of the townspeople. The instrument so fascinated him that he determined to discover all its secrets, to become a master player, and to learn everything he could about its art, history, and literature.

The remarkable fact about Segovia is that he is entirely self-taught. But Segovia the teacher was relentlessly critical and Segovia the pupil painstaking and diligent. At the age of fourteen, already displaying formidable technique and musicianship, he presented his first public concert, in Granada. This debut was followed by appearances at Córdoba and Sevilla, and, within a few months, a concert at the Ateneo in Madrid. A year later he gave a series of fifteen consecutive concerts in Barcelona, the last at the *Palau de la Música Catalana*. And the endless chain of concerts began . . . a tour throughout Spain first; then, with the ending of the First World War, South and Central America. In 1924 came his Paris debut, a brilliant performance attended by distinguished critics, musicians, and other luminaries of the art world who were unanimous in their praise. As a result of this unqualified success, he was engaged to play in all the major capitals of Europe. In 1925 he toured the Soviet Union. Then, in 1928, he played in New York for the first time and shortly afterward toured the entire Far East. In a few years he was known throughout the world.

In 1936, Segovia was acclaimed honorary president of the Society of the Classic Guitar in New York. In 1963 the University of Santiago de Compostela, Spain, conferred on him the degree doctor of philosophy and letters, honoris causa, and in 1969 the Florida State University at Tallahassee awarded him the degree doctor of music, honoris causa. Numerous other honors have been conferred upon him throughout his career, a career which has flourished without interruption beginning with that first concert in Granada.

Today, after more than sixty years on the concert stage, Andrés Segovia is at the peak of his intellectual and musical powers. At a recent concert a comment was overheard: "He is the grand-daddy of them all!"

And indeed he is!

the Segovia technique

31

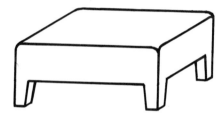

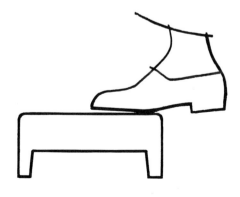

The classic playing position as practiced by Andrés Segovia offers the most secure support for the instrument and allows complete freedom of movement for the hands in order that execution may be relaxed and yet precise and perfect. Segovia uses a chair without arms, sitting on the front part of the seat. His body leans slightly forward, and the face of his guitar is held on a vertical plane, permitting him to see only the *edge* of the fingerboard and the sixth string. If Segovia needs to see the full fingerboard, he bends his head forward to look at it—without changing the position of the guitar. Segovia uses a flat footstool (five to six inches high) positioned in front of the left chair leg. The front part of his left foot rests on the near edge of the footstool, leaving his heel in the air (see illustration). This position allows a certain amount of flexibility in the left foot and leg. His right foot is placed slightly back and to the right of the right chair leg; the foot is supported by toes and ball of foot; it is not flat on the floor. The instrument is supported at four points: the right thigh, the left thigh, the underside of the right arm, and the chest. The incurved bout of the guitar rests on the left thigh. The right upper arm rests on the broadest part of the guitar body, leaving the forearm hanging completely free. To check if you have positioned your own right arm properly, swing your forearm in pendulum-like motion from the elbow without exerting any muscular effort for its support. If you can do that, your position most likely will be correct and will bring the right hand into the most favorable playing position relative to the strings (see page 34).

Segovia's left upper arm hangs vertically from the shoulder, allowing his left elbow to be as close to the body as *comfortably* possible. This eliminates a necessity of muscular effort to support the upper arm and contributes to the general relaxation of the body. The peghead of the instrument is at about the height of the collar bone. This orients the neck of the guitar at an angle of about thirty degrees with the horizontal as the most favorable playing position. Do not raise the left shoulder; keep it in a natural relaxed position.

The entire purpose of a good playing position is to give the player a relaxed yet alert posture, permitting a spatially precise orientation for confident execution.

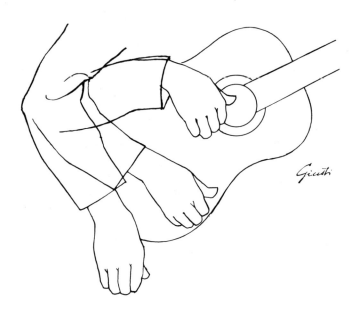

side view

While posing to illustrate
the importance of maintaining the face of the guitar
on a vertical plane, Segovia interrupted
for a moment. "Bobri," he said, tapping his
paunch, "caution the students to curb their appetites.
Otherwise, like me, they will have difficulty
in leaning sufficiently forward."

ladies playing position

A modified position for ladies
is recommended by the maestro.
Demonstrated by Señora Emilia Segovia,
herself an accomplished guitarist

With a shorter skirt

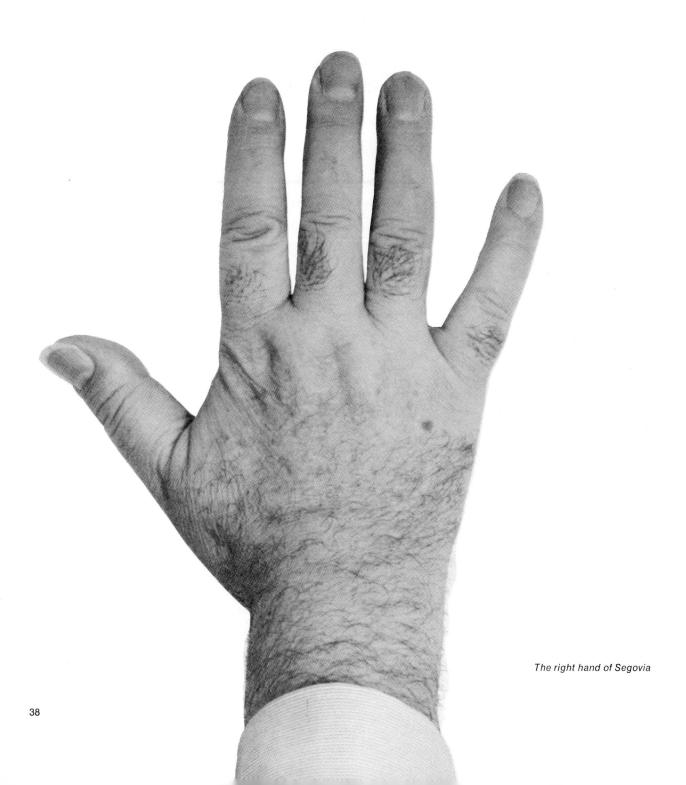

The right hand of Segovia

the right hand

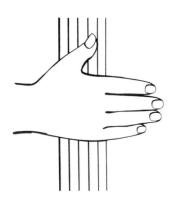

The classic position of the right hand, and for that matter the entire playing position, was evolved to achieve both beauty of tone and the utmost in relaxation while playing, thus enabling the performer to devote his attention entirely to the artistic aspects of his performance. Assuming that the position of the right upper arm and forearm is correct, the hand, *if completely relaxed,* will hang naturally in a position correct for playing: bent at the wrist, allowing the fingers to be at almost a right angle to the strings (with the knuckles parallel to them). Beginners usually find this position difficult to maintain while playing, mainly because they have a tendency to grow tense and "freeze" the wrist and arm. Complete relaxation with no muscular effort is the cure. A glance at two diagrammatic drawings on this page should make clear the essential difference between the correct and a faulty position of the hand in relation to the strings. It also will be clear that the most efficient delivery of the finger stroke to the strings will occur using the correct position, while the incorrect position can only result in a glancing blow, producing a weak tone.

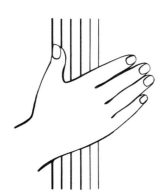

The side view of Segovia on page 35 illustrates the correct angle of the fingers and wrist. The right hand is held with the wrist arched, allowing a distance of from three to four inches between the inner side of the wrist and the soundboard. This gives an angle of about eighty degrees between the fingers and the strings. This *almost vertical* position of the tip and middle joints of the fingers in relation to the strings is of paramount importance in *tone production.* A finger stroke from this angle produces tone of great clarity and force.

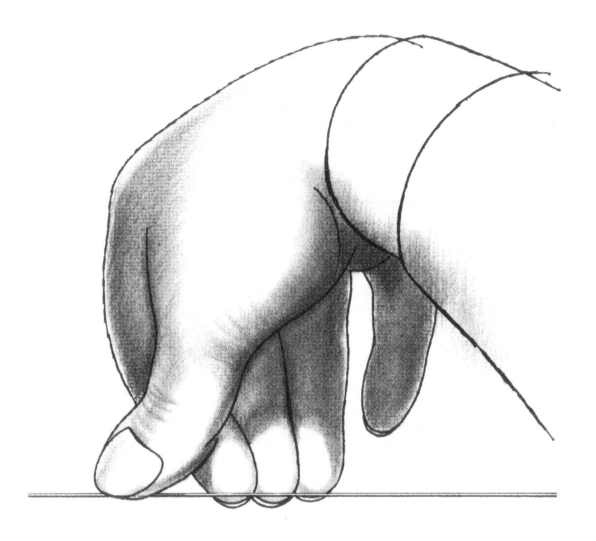

A careful study of these two illustrations of Segovia's right hand reveals several important elements. The thumb forms a cross with the index finger, presenting a triangular open space (a), and placing the index, middle, and annular fingers at an angle to the strings (leaning toward the fingerboard), the small finger being held vertically.

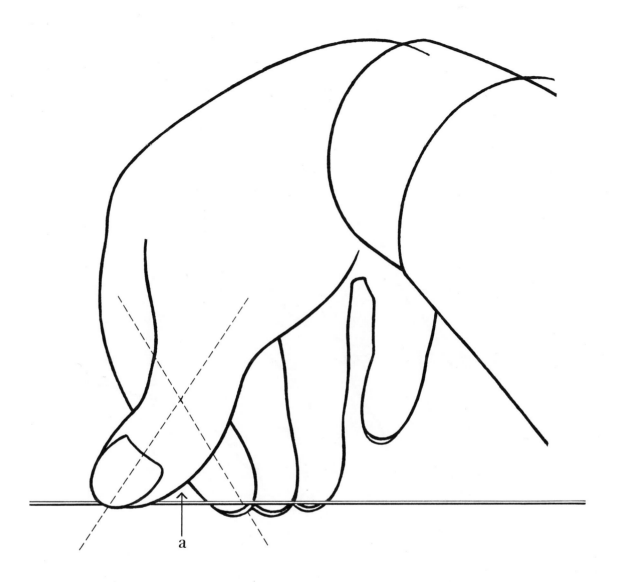

a

This hand position enables the player to use correctly the two principal methods of plucking the strings: the *apoyando,* sometimes referred to as a supported stroke, and the *tirando,* known as the free stroke. (Two other important techniques—pizzicato and harmonics—require special hand positions, described on pages 70, 72, and 73.)

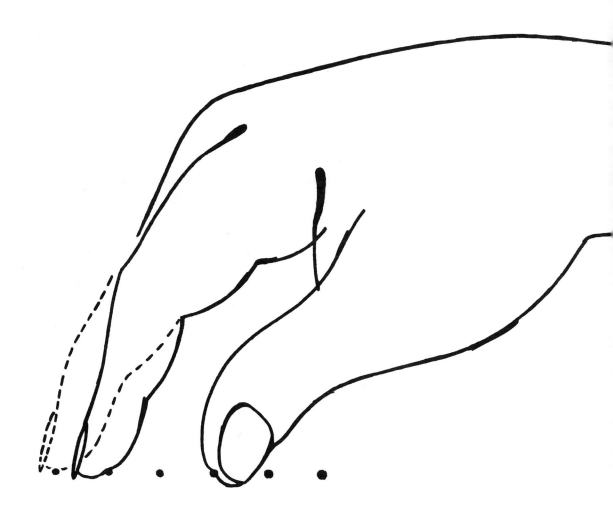

the apoyando stroke

This stroke, which contributed so much to revolutionizing the technique of our time, is achieved by plucking the strings with the first, second, or third finger, which after completing the stroke is brought to rest on the next string. This technique of striking the string enables the player to produce a greater volume of sound and gives more security and firmness by providing an additional point of support. It also increases the range of tonal shading, permits the fuller use of the resources of the instrument, and gives a clearer definition to the phrasing. The *apoyando* stroke is used principally for scale passages, essential notes of melody, and generally for all notes *not* forming part of a chord or arpeggio. In scales and melodic passages one should always alternate the fingers, avoiding repeated action of the same finger.

The introduction of the *apoyando* stroke is usually credited to Francisco Tárrega. Emilio Pujol, the eminent Spanish guitarist and musicologist, has stated that when he questioned Tárrega as to whether he was the inventor of the *apoyando* stroke, the master answered, "No, Julián Arcas used it in rapid scale passages, but without establishing any fixed order of fingering."

The author is inclined to attribute the invention of the *apoyando* stroke to the Flamenco guitarists. In order to be heard above the "taconeos" and "palmas" while accompanying dancers and singers, they probably developed the perpendicular supported stroke for playing fast melodic passages. And since the thumb was extensively used, even for melodic passages, with a downward supported stroke movement, it would have been only a short step for them to adapt the same technique to the rest of the fingers. Segovia concurs in this interpretation of the origin of the *apoyando* stroke.

Regardless of its origin, it was Tárrega and ultimately Segovia who developed and rationalized this technique, culminating in the matchless liquid and powerful "Segovia" tone we all admire so much.

the apoyando stroke

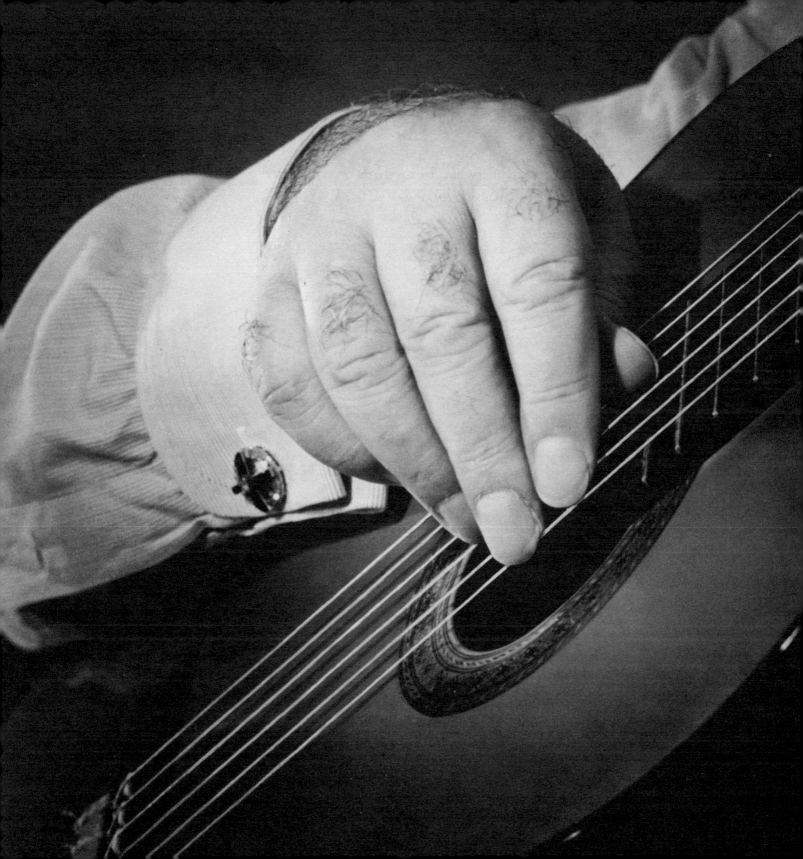

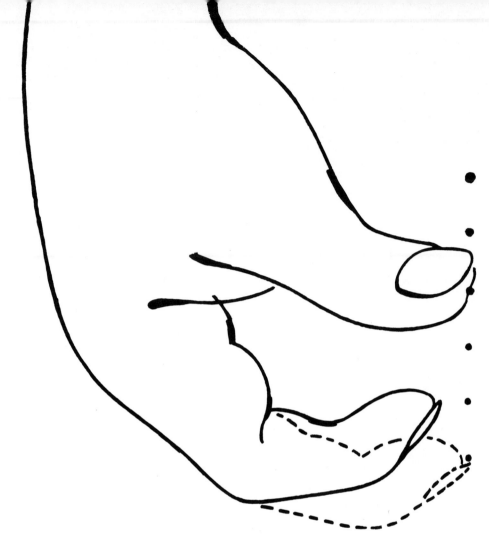

the tirando stroke

When Segovia executes the *tirando* stroke,

his fingers are held slightly more curved. The fingertip

describes a shallow arc toward the palm of the hand, and clears

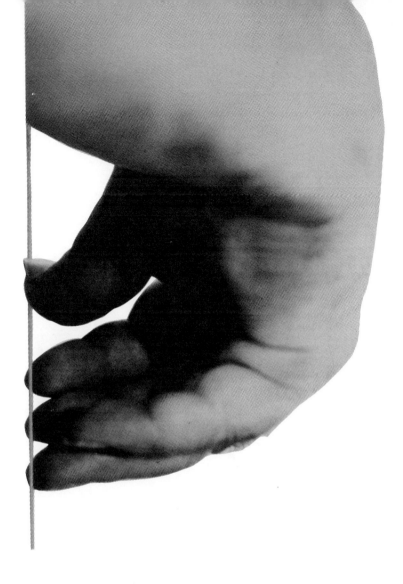

the next string instead of resting on it. This stroke is used in playing chords,

fast arpeggios, and in all instances when the neighboring

strings should vibrate simultaneously.

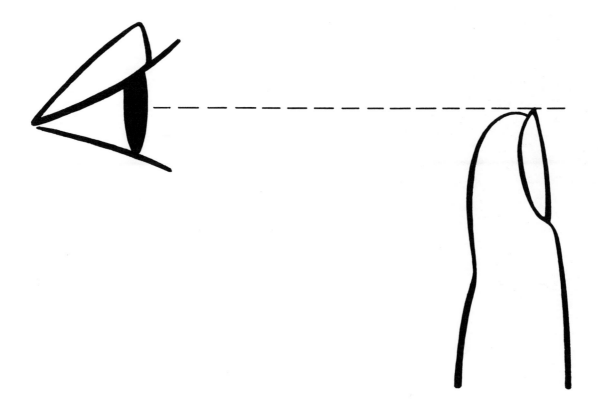

One cannot overemphasize the importance of properly trimmed nails in guitar playing. Segovia uses the nail alone or in combination with fingertip to produce sharp and metallic or soft and liquid tones, and all the variety of color and shading that he so masterfully evokes from the instrument. If one holds the right hand with the palm toward the face and the fingernails at eye level, the nails should be just long enough to be barely visible over the fingertips. Segovia expends great care on his nails, shaping

them daily to follow the *natural* contour of the fingertip, and polishing their edges with the finest abrasive paper. Some guitarists find a smooth piece of leather useful for rubbing a final polish to the nail edge.

The secret of producing a beautiful, yet powerful tone lies in the exact manner in which the nails are used. It is of utmost importance to strike the string at the point marked on the diagram (fig. 1). This point offers the opportunity to *start* the tone production with the *flesh* of the left side of the fingertip and ter-

48

nails—care and playing position

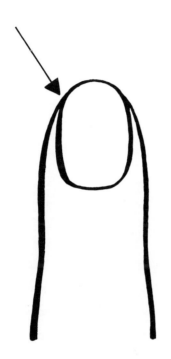

minate it with the nail, with a *minimum transition* from one to the other (fig. 1). If you examine your fingers (providing the nails are trimmed correctly), you will readily perceive that the *distance* between the nail edge and the tip of the finger is greater at the center point, gradually diminishing toward the left and right sides of the nail (see diagrams on this page). Holding the fingers at an angle to the strings enables you to contact the strings with your fingers *naturally,* at the point shown on the diagram (fig. 1).

Striking the string with the center point of the nail edge will result in a sharper, more metallic sound because of the longer "jump" from flesh to nail (fig. 2). This technique sometimes can be used to advantage for special effects of tone color variation. In fast arpeggio and tremolo passages the *nails alone* are usually the sound-producing agent.

right hand thumb technique

The proper use of the thumb is of paramount importance. Its misuse not only will adversely affect its own action but might considerably interfere with the free action of the fingers, or, worse, impart a rocking movement to the hand, impairing its security. The hand should at all times be as steady as possible, moving from the wrist without disturbing the position of the arm, allowing only the thumb and fingers to move. Segovia's hand appears motionless even during the fastest passages. Segovia's thumb is well advanced in the direction of the peghead *away* from the fingers *and at no time lodges behind* the fingers, since this would seriously interfere with finger motion (refer to the drawings on pages 40 and 41 and the photograph on page 51). He moves the thumb only from the *second joint* without bending the first (tip) joint or moving the hand. As seen clearly in the photograph, Segovia uses the outside edge or corner of the thumb, allowing the same smooth transition from flesh to nails as with the rest of the fingers. *Occasionally,* for special emphasis or tone color, Segovia uses the more central part of the thumb nail. Sometimes in order to produce a strong vibrating tone on the bass strings to emphasize the melody, his entire hand and forearm are used to impart additional momentum to the thumb stroke, yet hand and forearm are relaxed. This, we repeat, is for special effects only, and normally only his thumb and fingers move, without disturbing the position of the hand and forearm.

thumb poised to play

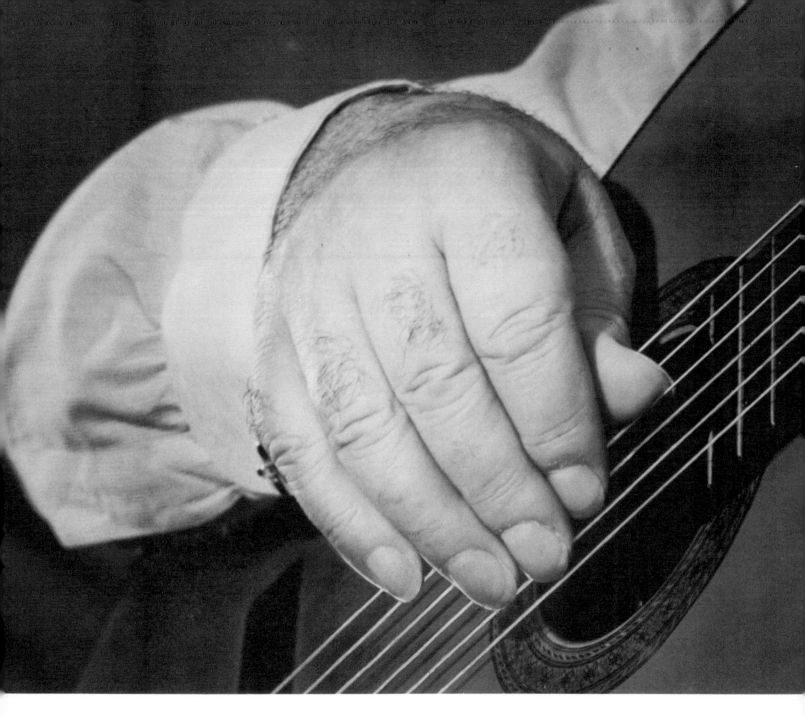

While the fingers are playing melodic passages from treble strings
to bass or vice versa, Segovia's thumb follows the fingers, lightly

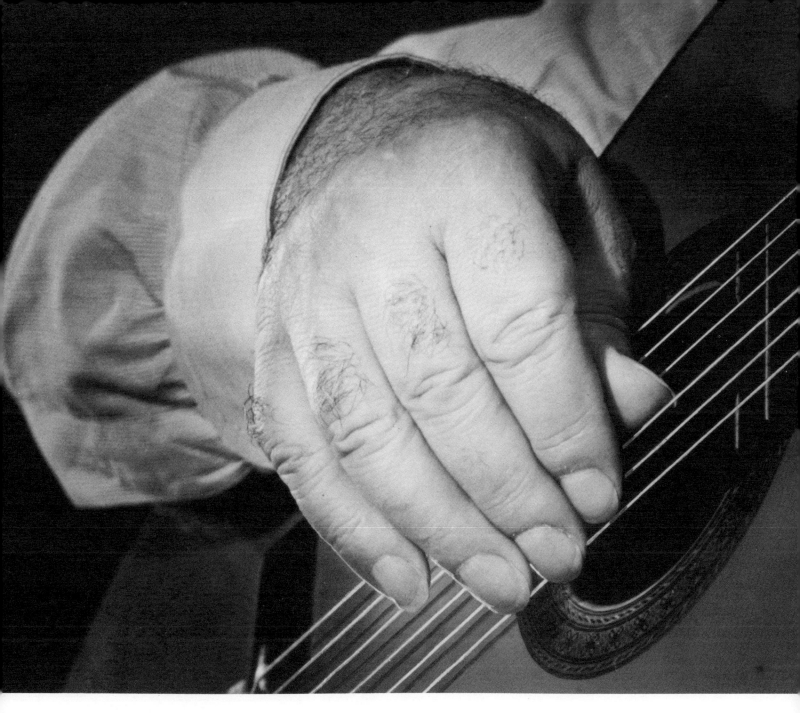

gliding on the strings (as can be seen in three successive photo-

graphs on pages 52, 53, and 54), and is not anchored on one of the

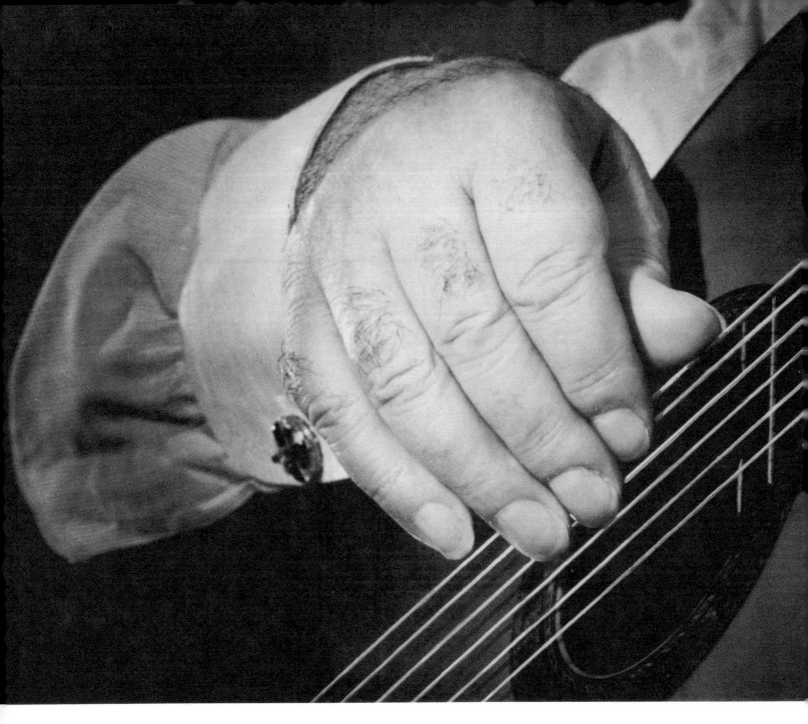

bass strings, because during these passages the elevation of the

wrist will be constantly changing, altering the angle of finger attack.

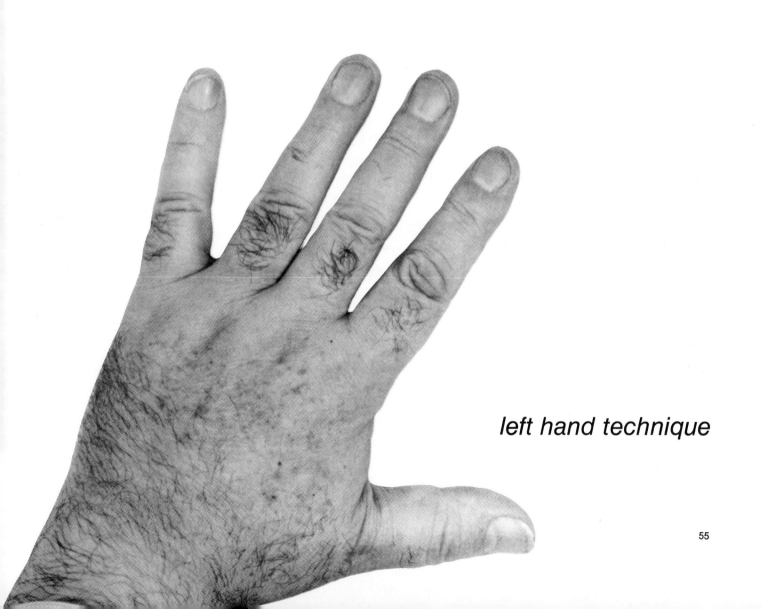

left hand technique

wrist and fingers

The secure manner in which the classic guitarist cradles his instrument obviates any need whatsoever for supporting the neck of the guitar with the left hand. Thus it is completely free for its proper function: the depression of the strings to the fingerboard. The fingers are more or less separated, depending on the notes they must play on the fingerboard, and are supported by the counter-pressure of the thumb on the back of the neck. Segovia's wrist is bent naturally and his fingers gracefully curved, in such a manner as to allow the first finger joint to press the string with a *perpendicular* action of the *tip* of the finger. Segovia files the nails of the left hand below the tips of his fingers, so they will not interfere with the pressure of his fingertips on the strings. (See page 55.) A common mistake with beginners is to hold the fingers insufficiently arched, pressing the strings with the soft pad of the finger instead of its firmer tip. The student is advised to be very careful not to fall into this bad habit.

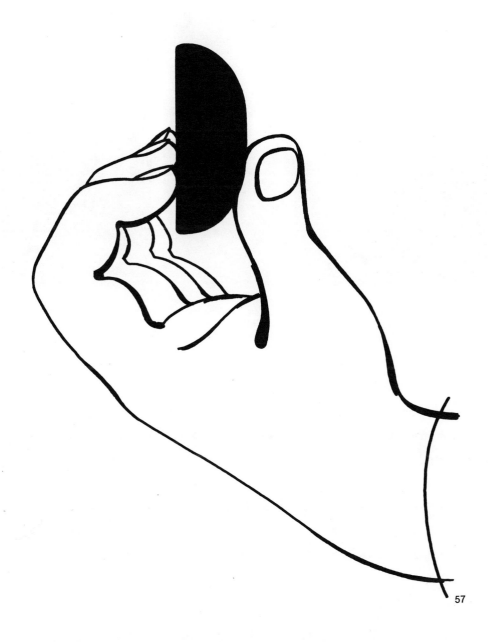

Fingers on the fingerboard.

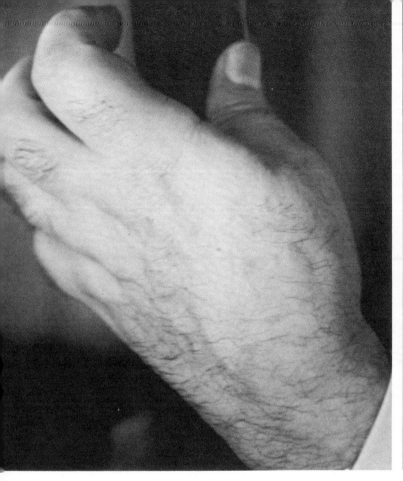 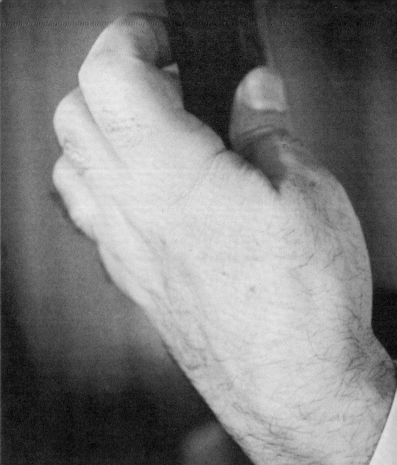

The fingers should be allowed to fall onto the finger-board from a *minimum elevation* above the strings; raising the fingers too high will result in loss of time, slowing the execution of fast passages. The strings are pressed as close as possible to the fret wire. This contributes greatly to the clarity and duration of the tone and prevents possible buzzing of the string.

Segovia uses only enough pressure to obtain a clear tone, without unduly squeezing the neck between the thumb and the fingers. His hand glides easily in a relaxed posture from one position to the other. He cautions that too much pressure will slow this movement, impede the execution, and tire the thumb.

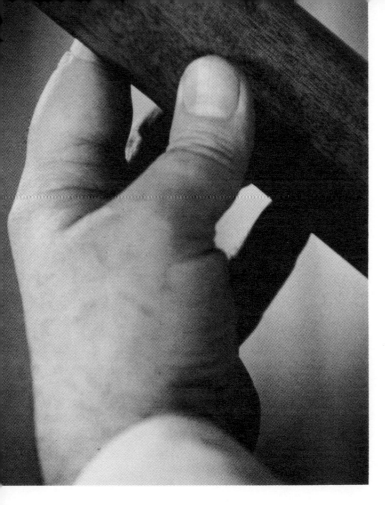

the left hand thumb

The sole role of the

left hand thumb is to provide

a counter-force to oppose the pressure of the fingers

on the fingerboard, never to support the weight of the neck.

The optimum position of the thumb is opposite the

second or third finger.

_____

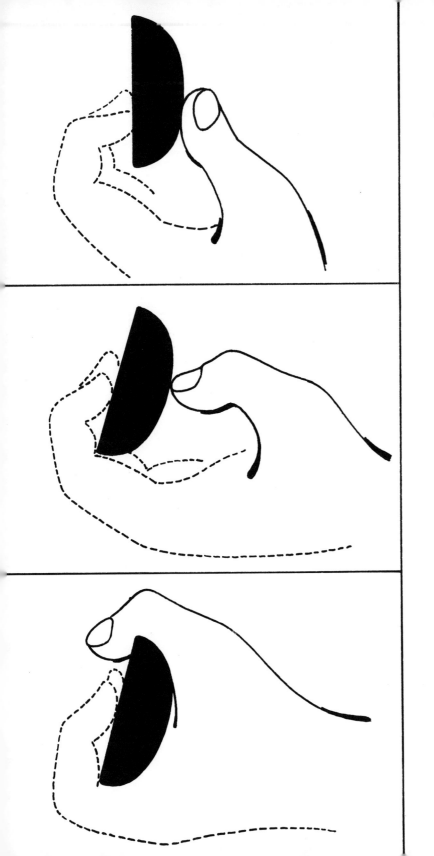

Segovia's thumb is slightly bent backward,
and the inner side of the fleshy pad is in contact with
the neck of the instrument, never the thumb tip.

Do not ever bend the thumb forward, using its tip
—or worse, the nail!

Cradling the neck between the thumb and first finger
is fatal to the development of correct technique:
its sole redeeming feature is to provide
instant recognition of a player's incompetence.

The point where the thumb touches the back of the neck
varies as the hand moves over the fingerboard,
but the bass side of the neck is forbidden territory.

While playing in the higher positions,
the thumb moves toward
the treble side of the instrument.

The student is advised to keep the thumb
opposite the second or third finger, where it will provide
a maximum counter-force to all four fingers equally.

61

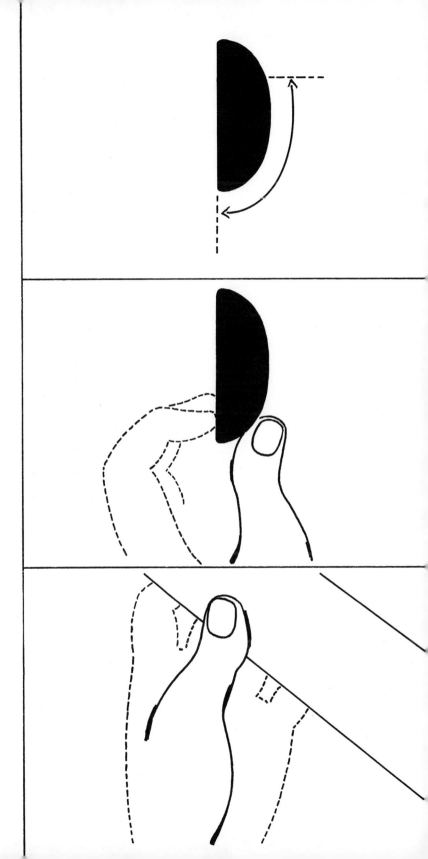

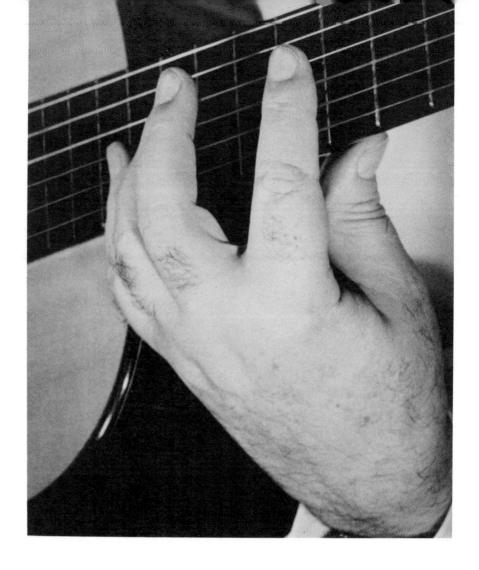

When Segovia plays in the higher positions (beyond the 12th fret), his thumb gives support to the fingers by resting on the treble *edge* of the fingerboard. The practice of leaving the fingers unsupported with the thumb hanging in the air while playing in the highest positions should be discouraged. Study of the maestro's left hand technique reveals that one can reach frets 12 to 19 without contortions, in a natural and graceful manner. Note the position of the thumb at the *edge* of the fingerboard in the photograph above.

barré technique

The barré is a technique of depressing simultaneously all six strings of the guitar with the left hand first finger. Usually it is indicated by a symbol C (Spanish *ceja*) and a Roman numeral to indicate the fret: as C VII. If fewer than six strings are to be depressed, the *half barré* is used, and the symbol is ½C, or ¢, plus the Roman numeral fret indication.

The thumb is *never* used in barring the bass strings. This is a sure sign of the player's technical ignorance or incompetence, or both. The use of the thumb in such a manner would effectively impede the correct action of the other left hand fingers.

The barré is produced by placing the first finger immediately behind the tone-producing fret. In studying Segovia's hand holding a barré on page 66, do not be misled by the first finger's appearing to press directly over the fret. The maestro's fingers are well developed and cushiony, and the first finger only seems to press on the fret, but the real pressure is immediately behind the fret. This photograph is very instructive, as it shows how *close* to the fret one should apply the pressure. In holding the barré, bend the finger backward slightly so the third joint is higher than the tip joint. This stretches the skin on the under side of the finger and presents a *firmer* surface for depressing the strings (page 66), resulting in a clearer tone with less force applied.

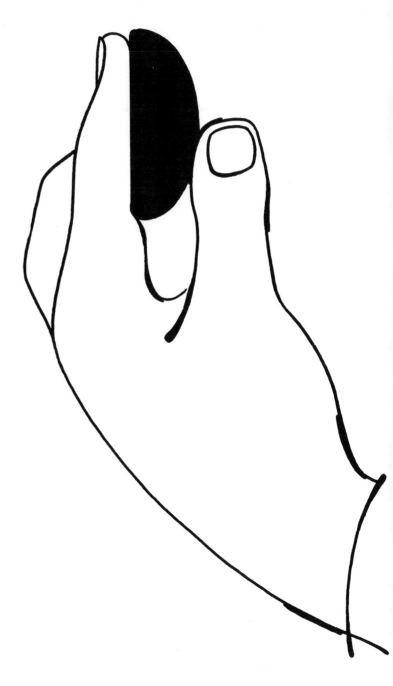

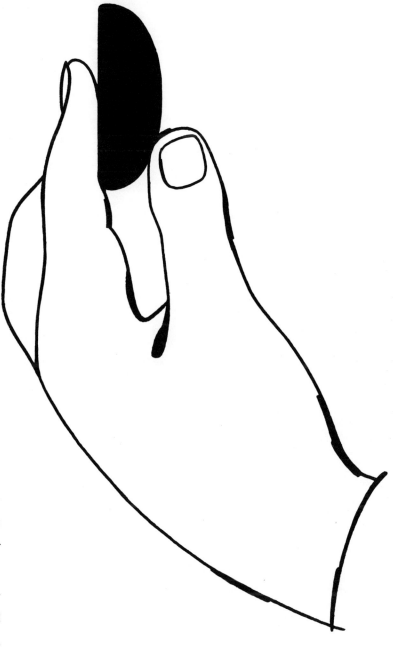

For the half barré, the position of the first finger is modified. The tip joint is bent, as shown in the photograph
on page 67. The common mistake is to bend the finger
at the second joint, instead of the tip joint.

The proper way of playing the barré will require considerable practice, but the beginner will be well advised
not to over-practice and to avoid over-tiring the muscles.

Occasionally other fingers might be used for barring
several strings.

65

barré

66

partial barré

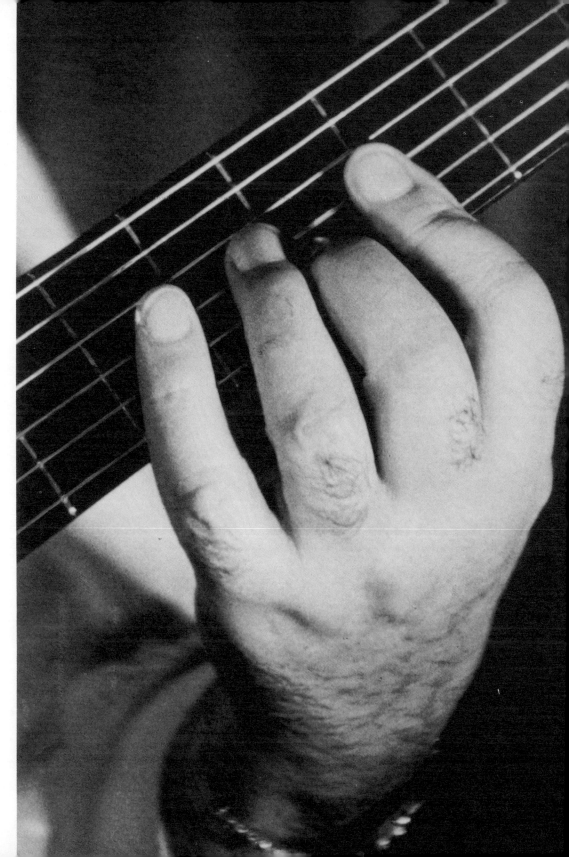

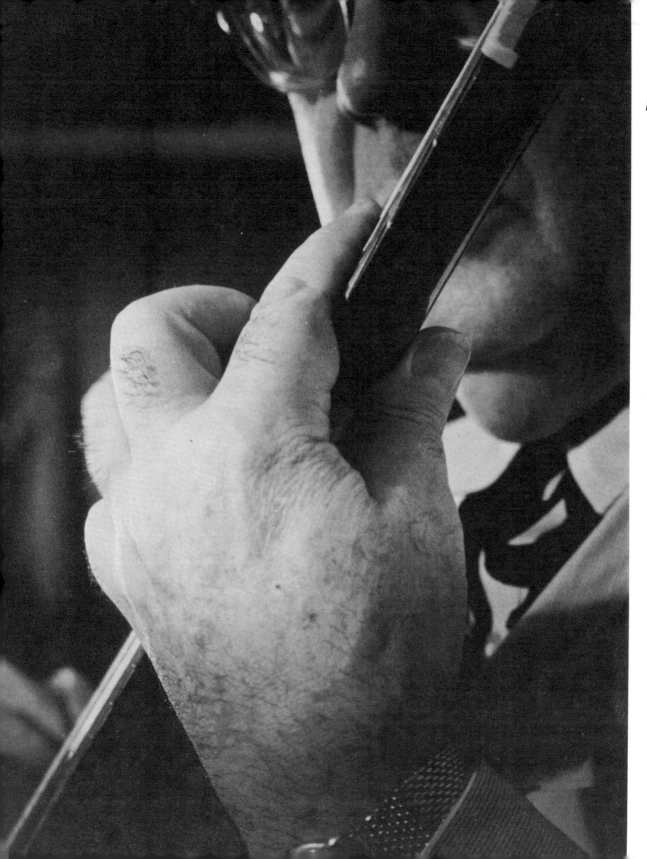

barré

partial barré

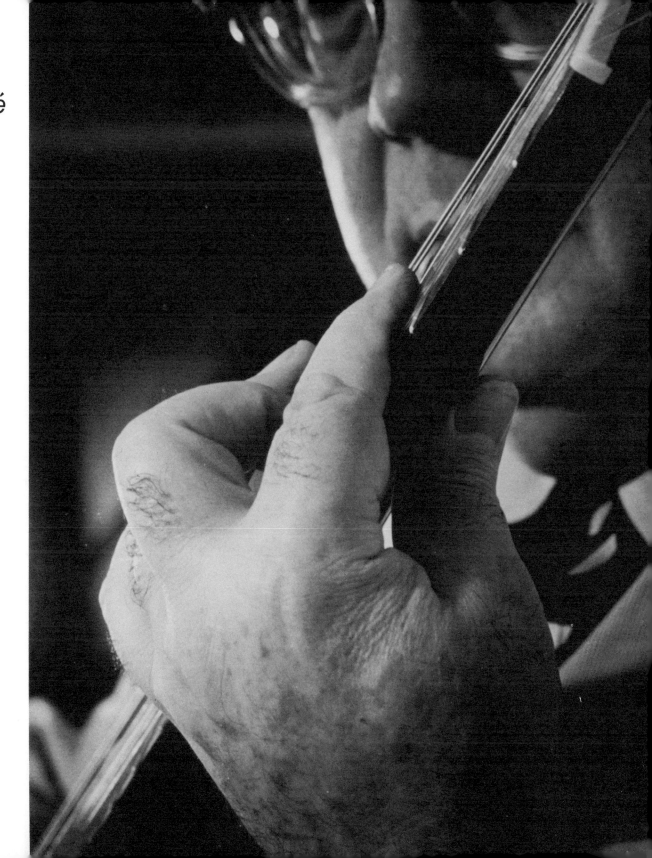

pizzicato stroke *(apagado, étouffé)*

To obtain this sound effect, similar to the muffled and short-sounding plucked notes obtained on the bowed instruments, the outer edge of the right hand is placed *lightly* over the bridge, covering also part of the strings immediately adjacent to the bridge bone. This acts as a damper comparable to the action of the left pedal on keyboard instruments, damping the vibration of the strings. The sound is produced by the action of the thumb (do not use the nail), and sometimes with the first finger, the other fingers resting lightly on the soundboard.

Segovia occasionally uses the soft inner part of the thumb (see diagram) for instant dampening of bass strings.

In discussing the pizzicato stroke, the maestro suggested that the Spanish word *apagado* (muffled) should be adopted by composers to indicate this particular *guitaristic* effect—in preference to the word *pizzicato*.

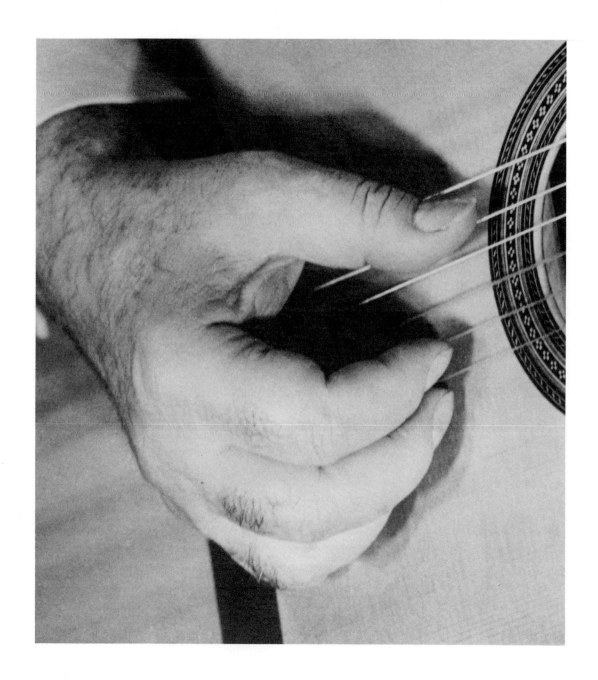

natural harmonics

The harmonics, or bell tones, are produced by lightly and momentarily touch-
ing the string *directly over a fret* with the left hand finger, without pressing
it to the fingerboard, and plucking with the right hand fingers at the same
time. The right hand fingers should strike the string at a point somewhere
nearer to the bridge than usual. This produces a clearer sounding harmonic.
This technique produces a clear, music box-like sound an octave or more
above the sound produced by the open string. Only certain frets can be used
in producing *natural* harmonics. Harmonics produced on frets 5, 7, and 12
are the clearest; those produced on frets 3, 4, 9, and 16, while practical, produce a somewhat less distinct sound.

octave harmonics *(artificial harmonics, harm. 8)*

To augment the limited range of the natural harmonics, another technique, *octave harmonics,* sometimes called *right hand harmonics,* can be used. This offers a much greater coverage of chromatic compass, and, while the sonority of the harmonics is somewhat less, there is an advantage of greater uniformity of tone and truer pitch. This technique requires *simultaneous* use (on the same string) of a left hand finger, the right hand index finger, and the right hand third finger. The left hand finger presses the string to the fingerboard in the usual way and *remains pressed down during the intended duration of sound.* The right hand index finger *gently and momentarily* touches the string at exactly halfway between the left hand fingered fret and the bridge bone. (This point is found 12 frets, or one octave, higher than the left hand fingered fret. For example, playing F on the first fret on the first string, the harmonic will be found precisely at fret 13.) The right hand third finger actually plucks the string.

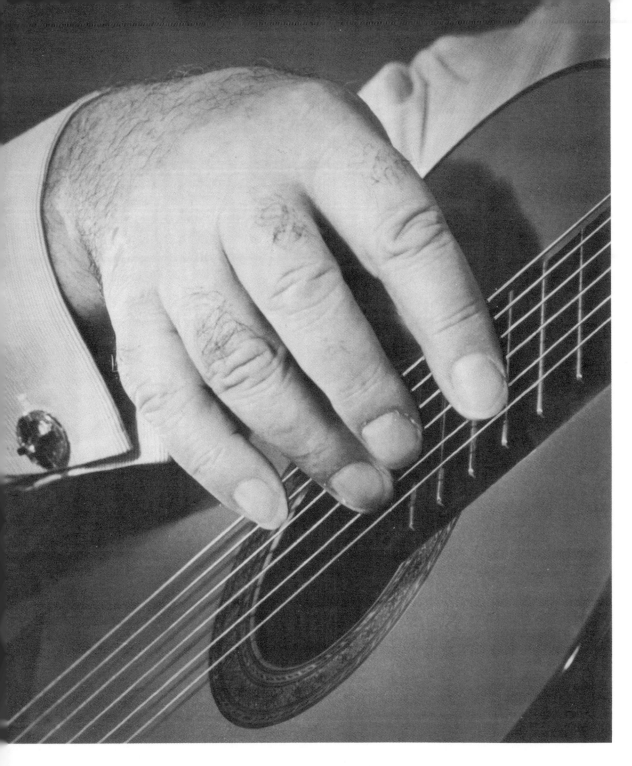

*artificial
harmonics*

74

epilogue

The nineteenth century, as we have already stated, could be considered the Golden Age of the Guitar. Aguado, Sor, Carcassi, Giuliani, and Carulli held audiences spellbound by the virtuosity of their performances. Enthusiastic listeners, duly impressed, directed their steps toward music shops, bought guitars and instruction books, and contracted for lessons. "Professors" of the guitar busily taught, and thousands nursed sore fingertips and prayed for calluses. The world, very much like today, was in the grip of guitaromania. History repeats itself.

The present-day renaissance of the classic guitar can be largely credited to the untiring efforts of Andrés Segovia. Segovia's appeal also inspired the lead taken by the Society of the Classic Guitar of New York in bringing together enthusiasts of the guitar and encouraging the formation of the hundreds of similar groups across the United States and in other countries. Segovia's marvelous technique, a logical development of the classic tradition, his uncanny ability to compel large audiences to attune their ears to the comparatively small voice and subtle color variations of this miniature orchestra, and his impeccable taste in selecting his material are factors behind the preservation of the classic guitar, a handmade thing of beauty so far removed from the morass of folksy twanging, sentimental balladeering, and brutality of the electrified horned monsters. Today new experiments in guitar construction applying rational acoustical vibration theory and scientific measuring techniques offer much promise for an instrument of a greater dynamic range and new tonal depth.

With an increase in the dynamic range of the classic guitar and much broader attention to its music by contemporary composers, a considerable enhancement of its already extensive repertoire is in the offing. At the same time deeper researches into other musical sources, including lute tablature, are constantly uncovering new gems of man's vast heritage of music for plucked instruments.

Not even the playing technique for the classic guitar can be considered static. The present brief treatise sets down for history the technique derived from past virtuosity and brought to its fullest fruition by Andrés Segovia. But as new musical resources are tapped, both through more powerful new instruments and through new compositions exploring the scope of the classic guitar, further refinements of technique may be anticipated. Segovia himself has demonstrated the need to remain flexible, constantly refining his technique.

Like Segovia, who first studied diligently the thinking of Aguado, Sor, Tárrega, and other masters of the past before venturing to introduce his own innovations, today's guitarist aspiring toward real artistry and mastery of his instrument *must* acquire full comprehension and use of the traditional technique, before embarking on experimentation of his own.

The aim of this volume, therefore, is to preserve an indisputable record of this technique, as developed and practiced by Andrés Segovia, and to serve as a visual and textual guide in establishing a solid *foundation* for playing technique by aspiring students. The science of the twentieth century has made it possible to record aurally, and in still and motion photography, the performances of great artists. The cultural contribution and perspicacity of Decca Records in recording Segovia playing the major part of his repertoire cannot be overestimated. We hope that this visual documentary will also prove to be a useful source of information for future researchers and historians about the development of the classic guitar in the second half of the twentieth century and about its foremost exponent, Andrés Segovia.

In addition, this book is homage to the great artist who inspired it. The reader will understand, then, that in focusing attention on details of Segovia's technique, I do not wish to imply that technique alone has been responsible for the miracle that is Segovia. For his technique, though prodigious, is merely the tool that enables his genius of musical taste and artistry of expression to soar unhindered.

Vladimir Bobri
25 december 1970

appendix

avoid these bad habits

Faulty position of right upper arm.

Right hand knuckles are not parallel to strings.

Right hand not sufficiently arched.

Left leg unsupported by footstool, causing improper

cradling of instrument.

Torso and head not sufficiently forward.

Left hand and fingers not arched; thumb on fingerboard

or extending above it.

Guitar held too horizontally (except in sketch number 2);

peghead not sufficient elevated.

In sketches 1, 2, and 3 soundboard not on vertical plane.

In sketches 1, 2, and 4, the barré is taken with

thumb and first finger; fingers not arched.

1

2

3

4

Giusti

methods and instruction books

The number of guitar methods and instruction books displayed on the counters of music stores today is staggering, and it is no wonder that bewildered beginners have to rely on the advice of a salesman seldom qualified to give it. The result is wasted effort, time, and money. In the preface to this book, Andrés Segovia gives us a clue to his preferences in teaching material. Aguado, Sor, Giuliani, Carulli, Tárrega, and later Villa-Lobos are the names mentioned. Accordingly, to help the student, a list of original editions of these masters that can be consulted in music libraries and some of the worthwhile contemporary revised editions obtainable today is presented. Besides the methods, we have included selected studies by these composers which are available today in modern editions, a few contemporary methods which the author considers to be useful for students, and books dealing with the history, construction, and technique of the guitar.

DIONISIO AGUADO (1784–1849)

This great virtuoso was not a prolific composer, but his published work leaves no doubt of his musicality. *Three Brilliant Rondos,* op. 16, alone are sufficient to establish him as a composer of taste and charm. His greatest contribution is his method, which was used as a study guide by many guitarists, including Segovia, in their formative years. Today, one hundred and forty-five years after its first publication, Aguado's method is as valid and indispensable for guitar as are the etudes of Kreutzer for violin or Czerny for the piano. Among the earliest editions we find *Escuela de Guitarra,* published by Fuentenebro, Madrid, 1825 (Sp.). A French translation was published by Massede in Paris (no date) and in 1827 by Richault, Paris, titled *Nouveau Méthode pour la guitare.* Another French edition entitled *Grande Méthode pour la guitare* issued by Lemoine in Paris bears no date. In 1843, D. Berito Campo, Madrid, published *Nuevo Método para Guitarra,* which included the well known portrait of Aguado using his invention, a "tripodion" to support the guitar (see page 16). Concert guitarist and teacher R. Sainz de la Maza carefully edited Aguado's *Método de Guitarra,* published by Union Musical Española in Madrid, 1943 (Sp.). Still another edition, *Gran Método Completo de Aguado,* revised by Argentine guitarist-composer A. Sinópoli, is obtainable from Ricordi-Americana, Buenos Aires (Sp.).

FERDINANDO CARULLI (1770–1841)

Usually considered one of the most important guitarists of the nineteenth-century Italian school, Ferdinando Carulli wrote a very popular method still reprinted today. The earliest copy appears to be his *Méthode pour la Guitare,* op. 241, published in 1810 by Carli in Paris (Fr.). A considerably enlarged sixth edition was published by Launer, Paris (Fr.). Some time later Polish guitarist J. N. Bobrowicz, pupil of Giuliani, revised and augmented the Launer edition. His version was published in German by Breitkopf & Härtel, Leipzig, in 1832. An Italian translation by Pietro Casati, published by Lucca in Florence in 1858 and, subsequently by Ricordi in Milan in 1896, is still being reprinted. More recent editions have been issued by Koster (Berlin, 1919), by Hofmeister (Leipzig, 1920), by Weinberger (Vienna, 1925), and by C. F. Peters (Leipzig, 1930).

FERNANDO SOR (1778–1839)

An important and internationally known musical personality during his lifetime, Fernando Sor was the only guitarist to perform with the London Philharmonic Society during the first hundred years of its existence. He is responsible for more than three hundred works, among them ballets, operas, melodramas, songs, oratorios, works for piano, chamber music, symphonies, military bands, as well as his numerous compositions for the guitar, which are always in good taste and display a superb knowledge of the technicalities of the instrument. Among them are to be found several small masterpieces extensively performed today and likely to be heard for years to come. Among other pedagogical works his *Méthode pour la guitare,* with an extremely interesting and extensive text, reveals Sor's preoccupations not only with playing technique but with acoustical problems of the sonority and design of the instrument. The volume contains many drawings of hand positions, posture, finger action, and diagrams of guitar construction. This method must be considered as a most remarkable treatise, the result of forty years of observation and reflection. His keenly analytical mind probes minutely into all possible aspects of guitar playing. A copy of it, in French and German, in the Library of Congress, Washington, D. C., published by N. Simrock, Bonn, unfortunately bears no date. According to P. J. Bone, an English translation by Arnold Merrick of the first edition originally published in Spain was published by Robert Cocks, London, and printed by Fowler, Cirencester (date not stated). The celebrated guitarist-composer Napoleon Coste (1806–1883) is responsible for *Méthode complète pour la guitare par Ferdinand Sor rédigée et augmentée* published in Paris by Schonenberger (no date). An extensive collection of Sor studies and small pieces in seven volumes, edited by Carl Dobrauz, entitled *Vorbereitende Uebungen, Kleine Musikstücke und Etüden,* was published by V. Hladky in Vienna. Over twenty-five years ago Andrés Segovia chose twenty of the most effective and beautiful of the Sor etudes, solving fingering problems in a masterly and ingenious fashion. Practiced intelligently and with diligence they are certain to develop strength and flexibility in both hands and lead to better command of the instrument. Published by Edward B. Marks, New York, in 1945. A collection of graded *Sixty Short Pieces for Guitar,* edited by Sophocles Papas, a teacher of many years of experience, published by Columbia Music Company, Washington, D. C. (1967), are suitable for the first and second year student. Several other revised editions and selections of Sor etudes are to be found in catalogs of Simrock (Leipzig), Schott, Zimmermann (Leipzig), and Lemoine (Paris). Especially recommended are opuses 6, 24, 31, 35, and 44.

MAURO GIULIANI (1781–1829)

This great virtuoso left us a rich legacy of compositions. Incredible as it seems, taking into consideration his constant public appearances, he (like Sor) found time to write more than three hundred compositions, including several concertos, many studies, numerous quartets, quintets, solos, and a *Practical Method for the Guitar* (op. 1) in four volumes (Fr., Ital., Germ.), published during his life (before 1840) by Ricordi in Milan and by Peters in Leipzig. The indispensable *120 Daily Studies for the Right Hand* edited by V. Bobri was published in 1949 by Celesta Company, New York. At the suggestion of Andrés Segovia, in order to escape the monotony of playing in the key of C through all 120 studies and to give the student the additional opportunity for study by leading him through all the tonalities practical on the guitar while preserving all the Giuliani formulae for the right hand, a new edition under the title *130 Daily Studies for the Classic Guitar* (op. 11), by V. Bobri, was published by Franco Colombo, New York, 1968.

MATTEO CARCASSI (1792–1853)

A Florentine guitarist of great virtuosity, Matteo Carcassi was a contemporary of Carulli and proved to be a formidable rival of the aging master. A brilliant performer, he also introduced a new style of music. His numerous compositions, pleasing and melodious, are full of imagination and new technical ideas and greatly influenced the contemporary guitarists. His *Complete Method for the Guitar* (op. 59), dedicated to his pupils, is one of the best ever written for beginners. In the preface to the first edition Carcassi writes, "It is my intention to facilitate the study of the guitar by adapting a system, which is most clear, simple, and precise." And so it is. The Carcassi method was favored with universal circulation and was translated, revised, condensed, augmented, and mutilated by successive waves of editors of every nationality. *Matteo Carcassi Guitar Method* in three volumes (Fr., Eng.) published by Schott & Co. (London) is one of the reliable editions available today and is constantly being reprinted. Carcassi augmented his method with a volume of *Twenty-Five Melodic and Progressive Etudes,* op. 60, also unmercifully "edited." The editions fingered by Miguel Llobet, published by Spanish Music Center, New York, and Karl Scheit's edition of twelve etudes from op. 60, called *Matteo Carcassi Etüden für die Mittelstufe,* op. 60, Universal Edition, Vienna, 1954, are recommended.

FRANCISCO TARREGA (1852–1909)

This fabled master of the guitar was fanatically and unselfishly devoted to the rehabilitation of the *guitarra de concierto.* He created a new romantic repertoire, made masterly transcriptions of works of Chopin, Schumann, and Bach, and wrote many original etudes and preludes. Among them, and of greatest benefit to students, are *Complete Technical Studies* (1969) and *Complete Preludes* (1961), both edited by Karl Scheit, and published by Universal Edition, Vienna.

HEITOR VILLA-LOBOS (1887–1959)

The Chôros No. 1, available from Columbia Music Company, Washington, D.C. (1963), *Five Preludes* (1954), and *Twelve Etudes* (1953), Editions Max Eschig, Paris, of Heitor Villa-Lobos have become a part of today's guitar concert repertoire.

In addition, listed below is more material which I have found very helpful in my own teaching experience.

In the Preface of his *Diatonic Major and Minor Scales*, Andrés Segovia counsels, "The student who wishes to acquire a firm technique on the guitar should not neglect the patient study of scales, which will enable him to solve a great number of technical problems in a shorter time than the study of any other exercise." Available from Columbia Music Company, Washington, D. C., 1953.

Das Gitarrespiel by Bruno Henze, published by Mitteldeutscher Verlag Halle, in Saale, 1950. This is an excellent method in fifteen volumes with a superb collection of solos, duos, trios, and works for voice-guitar and recorder-guitar.

For beginners, *Lehr und Spielbuch für Gitarre* by Karl Scheit, published by Osterreichischer Bundesverlag, Vienna, OBV 1721 13. This contains very useful material carefully graded in difficulty. Reading in the higher positions is introduced in a painless way.

La Escuela de la Guitarra by Mario Rodriguez Arenas, in seven volumes, published by Ricordi, in Buenos Aires. Fifth Edition 1954.

Emilio Pujol's *Escuela Razonada de la Guitarra,* in three volumes, published by Ricordi Americana, 1960. A magnificent method, based on Tárrega's technical precepts.

Ferdinando Carulli, *Gitarreschule,* edited by Walter Götze, published by C. F. Peters, Leipzig, 1930.

The Fingerboard Workbook, a non-method for guitar by Andrew Caponigro, published by G. Schirmer, Inc., 1969. This is a new approach for fingerboard study and is very useful.

The Collier Quick and Easy Guide to Playing the Guitar by Frederick M. Noad, published by Collier Books, New York; Collier-Macmillan Ltd., London, 1963.

The Art and Times of the Guitar—An Illustrated History of Guitars and Guitarists by Frederic V. Grunfeld, published by The Macmillan Company, New York; Collier-Macmillan Ltd., London, 1969.

The Illustrated History of the Guitar by Alexander Bellow, published by Franco Colombo Publications, a Division of Belwin/Mills Publishing Corp., Rockville Centre, L. I., New York, 1970.

Students interested in the construction of guitars are referred to *Classic Guitar Construction* by Irving Sloane, published by E. P. Dutton & Co., Inc., New York, 1966, and *Guitar Review* 28: *Guitar Construction from A to Z,* published in 1965.

The Guitar Review, one of the most important sources of information concerning the classic guitar. Scholarly articles by international authorities on musicology, technique, construction, folklore music. Rare musical selections. Profusely illustrated. Luxuriously printed. Now published by Augustine Strings Inc., NYC.

photographs and illustrations

index

VLADIMIR BOBRI was born on 13 May 1898 in Kharkov, the Ukraine. In a family atmosphere of culture and scholarship, he acquired an adventuresome attitude toward life and art. He is a graduate of the Imperial Art School of Kharkov, where he became interested in the theater and in early ikon painting, and he studied scenic design by apprenticeship at the State Dramatic Theater. Because of the turbulent events of the Revolution, he fled from Russia in 1917, leaving his homeland forever. In Constantinople (Istanbul), he designed sets and costumes for the Russian ballet, produced movie posters, and painted ikons in a monastery; in Anatolia (Turkey), he engaged in archeological work. Then, in 1921, he settled in New York, where he has become known for his imaginative murals, advertising art, and book illustrations. Although Bobri is a painter, he has a secondary, almost equal love for music, especially for music of the guitar. In 1936, he was a founding member of the Society of the Classic Guitar, an organization that was to have a far-reaching influence on the growth of interest in the guitar in this country. Since 1948, he has been editor and art director of *The Guitar Review*. He is the author of many essays on subjects related to the classic guitar and has composed a number of works for the instrument.

by the same author

Danza en La
Celesta Publishing Company, NYC, 1936

Valor Gitano
Celesta Publishing Company, NYC, 1944

Sirocco (Tango)
Celesta Publishing Company, NYC, 1944

Adieu (Elegy)
Celesta Publishing Company, NYC, 1945

Coquetería (Waltz)
Celesta Publishing Company, NYC, 1945

Eight Melodic Exercises in the Form of Preludes
Franco Colombo, Inc., NYC, 1968

130 Daily Studies for the Classic Guitar
Franco Colombo, Inc., NYC, 1968

Very Easy Pieces for Very, Very Beginners
Franco Colombo, Inc., NYC, 1969

Complete Study of the Tremolo
Franco Colombo, Inc., NYC, 1971

The classic guitar is a difficult and demanding instrument. *There are no short cuts.* Beginners are strongly advised to start under the guidance of a *qualified* teacher. This will tend to prevent the formation of bad habits which beginners are almost certain to fall into and which are so difficult to correct later.

IMPORTANT PUBLISHER'S NOTE:

We have reissued THE SEGOVIA TECHNIQUE with not a word altered. It reads exactly as it did in 1972 when it was first published. Naturally some of the references have changed in the last eighteen years. My dear friends Vladimir Bobri and Martha Nelson are both dead, as is Andrés Segovia. The Society of the Classic Guitar no longer exists and *Guitar Review* is now published by the makers of Augustine Strings. With this in mind I asked Clare Callahan, Chairman of Classical Guitar Studies at the University of Cincinnati, College–Conservatory of Music, if she would prepare an up-to-date list of methods and instruction books. Her suggestions are listed below.   — NICHOLAS CLARKE.

STUDIES

Dionisio Aguado. *Twenty-four Studies*. Schott, 1928.
Leo Brouwer. *Études Simples* (4v). Editions Max Eschig, 1972.
Matteo Carcassi. *Twenty-five Studies*, Op. 60. Schott.
Napoleon Coste. *Twenty-five Studies*, Op. 38. Schott, 1926.
Stephen Dodgson & Hector Quine. *Studies for Guitar* (2v). Ricordi, 1965.
John Duarte. *Foundation Studies*. Novello, 1966.
Mauro Giuliani. *Twenty-four Studies*, Op. 48. Schott, 1926.
---------------------. *Metodo per Chitarra*, Op. 1. Berben, 1964.
Guglielmo Paparo. *La Technica degli Arpeggi*. Bergen, 1965.
Fernando Sor. *Twenty Studies* ed. by André Segovia. Marks.
Francisco Tárrega. *Complete Technical Studies*. Universal Edition, 1969.
Heitor Villa-Lobos. *Douze Études*. Editions Max Eschig, 1929.

METHODS

Dionisio Aguado. *New Guitar Method*. Tecla, 1981.
Abel Carlevaro. *Serie Didactica para Guitarra* (4v). Barry, 1966.
Charles Duncan. *A Modern Approach to Classical Guitar* (3v). Hal Leonard Publishing Corp., 1981.
Frederick Noad. *Solo Guitar Playing* (2v). Schirmer Books, 1976.
Emilio Pujol. *Escuela Razonada de la Guitarra* (4v). Ricordi, 1952. [English transl. of vol. 1-2 also published by Editions Orphée.]
Aaron Shearer. *Learning the Classical Guitar* (4v). Mel Bay Publications, 1990.

TEXTS

Charles Duncan. *The Art of Classical Guitar Playing*. Summy-Birchard, 1980.
Lee F. Ryan. *The Natural Classical Guitar*. The Bold Strummer, 1990.

Other Music Titles Available from The Bold Strummer, Ltd.

GUITAR

THE AMP BOOK: A Guitarist's Introductory Guide to Tube Amplifiers *by Donald Brosnac.*
ANIMAL MAGNETISM FOR MUSICIANS: Making a Bass Guitar and Pickup from Scratch *by Erno Zwaan.*
ANTONIO DE TORRES: Guitar Maker—His Life and Work *by José L. Romanillos. Fwd. by Julian Bream.*
THE ART OF FLAMENCO *by D. E. Pohren.*
THE ART OF PRACTICING *by Alice Artzt.*
CLASSIC GUITAR CONSTRUCTION *by Irving Sloane.*
THE FENDER GUITAR *by Ken Achard.*
THE FLAMENCO GUITAR, REISSUE *by David George.*
THE GIBSON GUITAR *by Ian C. Bishop.* 2 vols.
GUITAR HISTORY: Volume 1—Guitars Made by the Fender Company *by Donald Brosnac.*
GUITAR HISTORY: Volume 2—Gibson SGs *by John Bulli.*
GUITAR HISTORY: Volume 3—Gibson Catalogs of the Sixties *edited by Richard Hetrick.*
GUITAR REPAIR: A Manual of Repair for Guitars and Fretted Instruments *by Irving Sloane.*
THE HISTORY AND DEVELOPMENT OF THE AMERICAN GUITAR *by Ken Achard.*
AN INTRODUCTION TO SCIENTIFIC GUITAR DESIGN *by Donald Brosnac.*
LEFT HANDED GUITAR *by Nicholas Clarke.*
LIVES AND LEGENDS OF FLAMENCO, 2ND EDITION *by D. E. Pohren.*
MANUAL OF GUITAR TECHNOLOGY: The History and Technology of Plucked String Instruments *by Franz Jahnel. English vers. by Dr. J.C. Harvey.*
THE NATURAL CLASSICAL GUITAR, REISSUE *by Lee F. Ryan.*
THE SEGOVIA TECHNIQUE, REISSUE *by Vladimir Bobri.*
THE SOUND OF ROCK: A History of Marshall Valve Guitar Amplifiers *by Mike Doyle.*
THE STEEL STRING GUITAR: Construction and Repair, UPDATED EDITION *by David Russell Young.*
STEEL STRING GUITAR CONSTRUCTION *by Irving Sloane.*
A WAY OF LIFE, REISSUE *by D. E. Pohren.*

PIANO / HARPSICHORD

THE ANATOMY OF A NEW YORK DEBUT RECITAL *by Carol Montparker.*
AT THE PIANO WITH FAURÉ, REISSUE *by Marguerite Long.*
EUROPEAN PIANO ATLAS *by H. K. Herzog.*
GLOSSARY OF HARPSICHORD TERMS *by Susanne Costa.*
KENTNER: A Symposium *edited by Harold Taylor. Fwd. by Yehudi Menuhin.*
LIPATTI *by Dragos Tanasescu & Grigore Bargauanu.*
THE PIANIST'S TALENT *by Harold Taylor. Fwd. by John Ogdon.*
THE PIANO AND HOW TO CARE FOR IT *by Otto Funke.*
THE PIANO HAMMER *by Walter Pfeifer.*
PIANO NOMENCLATURE, 2ND EDITION *by Nikolaus Schimmel & H. K. Herzog.*
RAVEL ACCORDING TO RAVEL *by Vlado Perlemuter & Hélène Jourdan-Morhange.*

Other Music Titles Available from The Bold Strummer, Ltd. (continued)

SCHUBERT'S MUSIC FOR PIANO FOUR-HANDS *by Dallas Weekley & Nancy Arganbright.*
TECHNIQUE OF PIANO PLAYING, 5TH EDITION *by József Gát.*
THE TUNING OF MY HARPSICHORD *by Herbert Anton Kellner.*

See also:
  ALKAN (2 volumes) *(Smith).*
  LISZT AND HIS COUNTRY, 1869-1873 *(Legány).*
  PERCY GRAINGER: The Man Behind the Music *(Dorum).*
  PERCY GRAINGER: The Pictorial Biography *(Simon)..*
  RONALD STEVENSON: A Musical Biography *(MacDonald).*
  SORABJI: A Critical Celebration *(Rapoport).*
  A SOURCE GUIDE TO THE MUSIC OF PERCY GRAINGER *(Lewis).*
  TENSIONS IN THE PERFORMANCE OF MUSIC: A Symposium, REVISED & EXTENDED EDITION *(Grindea).*

BIOGRAPHIES & COMPOSER STUDIES

ALKAN, REISSUE *by Ronald Smith.* Vol. 1: The Enigma. Vol. 2: The Music.
BEETHOVEN'S EMPIRE OF THE MIND *by John Crabbe.*
BÉLA BARTÓK: His Life in Pictures and Documents *ed. by Ferenc Bónis.*
BERNARD STEVENS AND HIS MUSIC: A Symposium *compiled and edited by Bertha Stevens.*
JANÁCEK: Leaves from His Life *by Leos Janácek. Edited & transl. by Vilem & Margaret Tausky.*
JOHN FOULDS AND HIS MUSIC: An Introduction *by Malcolm MacDonald.*
LIPATTI *(Tanasescu & Bargauanu): see* PIANO, above.
LISZT AND HIS COUNTRY, 1869-1873 *by Deszo Legány.*
MASCAGNI: An Autobiography Compiled, Edited and Translated from Original Sources *by David Stivender.*
MAX REGER *by Gerhard Wuensch.*
MICHAEL TIPPETT, O.M.: A Celebration *edited by Geraint Lewis. Fwd. by Peter Maxwell Davies.*
THE MUSIC OF SYZMANOWSKI *by Jim Samson.*
MY LIFE WITH BOHUSLAV MARTINU *by Charlotte Martinu.*
THE OPRICHNIK: An Opera in Four Acts by Peter Il'ich Tchaikvoksy. *Transl. & notes by Philip Taylor.*
PERCY GRAINGER: The Man Behind the Music *by Eileen Dorum.*
PERCY GRAINGER: The Pictorial Biography *by Robert Simon. Fwd. by Frederick Fennell.*
RAVEL ACCORDING TO RAVEL *(Perlemuter & Jourdan-Morhange): see* PIANO, above.
RONALD STEVENSON: A Musical Biography *by Malcolm MacDonald.*
SCHUBERT'S MUSIC FOR PIANO FOUR-HANDS *(Weekley & Arganbright): see* PIANO, above.
SOMETHING ABOUT THE MUSIC 1: Interviews with 17 American Experimental Composers *by Geoff Smith & Nicola Walker.*
SOMETHING ABOUT THE MUSIC 2 *edited by Thomas P. Lewis.*
SOMETHING ABOUT THE MUSIC 3: Landmarks of Twentieth-Century Music *by Nick Rossi.*
SORABJI: A Critical Celebration *edited by Paul Rapoport.*
A SOURCE GUIDE TO THE MUSIC OF PERCY GRAINGER *edited by Thomas P. Lewis.*
THE SYMPHONIES OF HAVERGAL BRIAN: Symphonies 30-32, Survey, and Summing-Up *by Malcolm MacDonald.*
VERDI AND WAGNER *by Ernö Lendvai.*

Other Music Titles Available from The Bold Strummer, Ltd. (continued)

THE WORKS OF ALAN HOVHANESS: A Catalog, Opus 1–Opus 360 *by Richard Howard*.
ZOLTAN KODALY: His Life in Pictures and Documents *by László Eosze*.

GENERAL SUBJECTS

ACOUSTICS AND THE PERFORMANCE OF MUSIC *by Jürgen Meyer*.
AMERICAN MINIMAL MUSIC, REISSUE *by Wim Mertens. Transl. by J. Hautekiet*.
A CONCISE HISTORY OF HUNGARIAN MUSIC, 2ND ENL. ED. *by Bence Szabolozi*.
THE FOLK MUSIC REVIVAL IN SCOTLAND, REISSUE *by Ailie Munro*.
GOGOLIAN INTERLUDES: Gogol's Story "Christmas Eve" as the Subject of the Operas by Tchaikovsky and
 Rimsky-Korsakov *by Philip Taylor*.
THE MUSICAL INSTRUMENT COLLECTOR, REVISED EDITION *by J. Robert Willcutt & Kenneth R. Ball*.
A MUSICIAN'S GUIDE TO COPYRIGHT AND PUBLISHING, ENLARGED EDITION *by Willis Wager*.
MUSICOLOGY IN PRACTICE: Collected Essays by Denis Stevens *edited by Thomas P. Lewis*. Vol. 1: 1948-1970.
 Vol. 2: 1971-1988.
THE PRO/AM BOOK OF MUSIC AND MYTHOLOGY *compiled, edited & with commentaries by*
 Thomas P. Lewis.
THE PRO/AM GUIDE TO U.S. BOOKS ABOUT MUSIC: Annotated Guide to Current & Backlist Titles *edited by Thomas*
 P. Lewis. 2 vols.
SKETCHES FROM MY LIFE *by Natalia Sats*.

PERFORMANCE PRACTICE / "HOW-TO" INSTRUCTIONAL

GUIDE TO THE PRACTICAL STUDY OF HARMONY *by Peter Il'ich Tchaikovsky*.
HOW TO SELECT A BOW FOR VIOLIN FAMILY INSTRUMENTS *by Balthasar Planta*.
THE JOY OF ORNAMENTATION: Being Giovanni Luca Conforto's *Treatise on Ornamentation* (Rome, 1593) *with a*
 Preface by Sir Yehudi Menuhin and an Introduction by Denis Stevens.
THE MUSICIANS' THEORY BOOK: Reference to Fundamentals, Harmony, Counterpoint, Fugue and Form *by Asger*
 Hamerik.
THE STUDENT'S DICTIONARY OF MUSICAL TERMS.
TENSIONS IN THE PERFORMANCE OF MUSIC: A Symposium, REVISED & EXTENDED EDITION *edited by Carola*
 Grindea. Fwd. by Yehudi Menuhin.
THE VIOLIN: Precepts and Observations *by Sourene Arakelian*.